# An Animal of the Sixth Day

*para Mai,*
*Marta Consuelo Gaytan de Fargas,*
*abuelita, fondo, ejemplo de coraje—*
*"el que boca tiene, a Roma va."*

# An Animal of the Sixth Day

## Laura Fargas

Texas Tech University Press

This book was set in Garamond with Dauphin display and Caslon numbers and printed on acid-free paper that meets the Guidelines for permanence and durability of the Committee on Production Guidelines for Book Longevity of the Council on Library Resources.  (∞)

Printed in the United States of America.

Design by Ted Genoways

Jacket illustration The Sixth Day of Creation, from the twelfth-century Byzantine mosaic of the Creation in the Palatine Chapel of the Palazzo dei Normanni, Palermo, Sicily.  Color plate by Annibale Belli.

Library of Congress Cataloging-in-Publication Data
    Fargas, Laura.
        An animal of the sixth day / Laura Fargas.
            p.  cm.
        ISBN 0-89672-360-7 (alk. paper)
        I. Title.
    PS3556.A7138A5   1996
    811'.54—dc20                                              95-35941
                                                                 CIP


96 97 98 99 00 01 02 03 04 / 9 8 7 6 5 4 3 2 1

Texas Tech University Press
P.O. Box 41037
Lubbock, Texas 79409-1037 USA
1-800-832-4042

# Acknowledgments

Some of these poems first appeared in the following publications:

"An Animal Of The Sixth Day," "Doggy Doggerel," "Living In Is," "Wave & Particle," "'Winter, Leper of the World,'" and "Timshel" [as "Timshel: *Thou Mayest*"]   *The Georgia Review;*

"Irises"   *The Atlantic Monthly;*

"If there is a" and "Reflecting What Light We Can't Absorb"   *The Paris Review;*

"Psyche" and "Speaking"   *Poet Lore;*

"Grass The Fine Body Hairs Of Earth" and "Natural Selection" [as "Actively Speciating Even Now"]   *Poetry;*

"A Night When Only Angels Interest Me," "The Problem of Good," and "Translated as 'Experience' or 'Suffering'"   *Alaska Quarterly Review;*

"Canopy"   *Bulletin of the Catoctin Valley Canoe Club;*

"Absolute Location," "At Poplar Pond," "'The Battle for Peace Has Begun,'" "Barely Husbanding Their Own Bodies," "Between the angels" "The First Elegy," "Ode to Joy," "Palos Verdes High School," "Peris," "Stitch in Time," and "Valhalla," *Reflecting What Light We Can't Absorb* (Riverstone Press, 1993).

I am daily grateful to my friends, family, teachers, and colleagues for their good influences, good examples, and good wishes. I want to specially thank all the other members of The Poetry Group That Could Not Speak Its Name—Toi, BG, Judy, Elaine, Catherine, and Hilary—for those kind and wonderful roses. For constant help, I want to thank Barbara Goldberg, Jane Hirshfield, Elaine Magarrell and Catherine Harnett Shaw.

I also want to express deep gratitude for institutional support to Yaddo, where a significant number of these poems were written; the D.C. Commission on the Arts and Humanities, for grants that made writing time possible; and the OSH Division, Office of the Solicitor, U.S. Department of Labor, for allowing me to take that time, with particular thanks to Cynthia L. Attwood and Daniel J. Mick. This book and its poems have also benefitted greatly from the editorial support and suggestions of Stan Lindberg, Anita Jepson Gilbert, Judith Keeling, Ted Genoways, and Walter McDonald.

LF

Winners of the TTUP First-Book Competition in Poetry are selected by Poetry Editor Walter McDonald, who surveys some twenty literary journals throughout the year and invites normally one dozen poets to submit manuscripts for consideration in the competition.

The Competition has been supported generously this year through donated subscriptions from *American Scholar, Georgia Review, Poetry,* and *Southern Review.*

# Foreword

Laura Fargas' book begins, "You have certain rights." For me, her poems are like blessings to proceed. I like the voice, the spirit I find in her poems. She accepts and celebrates the rich possibilities and, even with the risks and limitations of it all, insists that living on this earth is splendid. When I first read *An Animal of the Sixth Day,* I scribbled these summary words: "Remarkably strong and beautiful poems; the implicit sub-title of her book is *Ode to Joy.*"

"These are the opposites of commandments," she writes in "Timshel," the opening poem—a beginning that makes a leap into possibility, claiming an amazing acceptance of self, a delicious freedom: "I may do / what I have done." (When I read that, I wrote in the margin, *"Ah!"*)

What an unfoldingly lovely book to read. She makes poems about angels and ordinary events so exciting, so lovable.

> I may mention to God now and then how much I love it all,
> remembering also how much I want. Please,
> I may say, this giddy greed is part of the gift.
> ("Timshel")

This habit of mind and spirit is generous, not often popular in a world so troubled. Her poems are breathtaking, beautiful—sensuous imagery, sounds she repeats for the pleasure of reading, the surprising juxtaposition of images that spark the insights. Consider, for example: "Timshel," the exciting opening poem (the poem that caused me to list her as one of the poets to invite); "Peris"; "Irises"; "October-struck"; "Ode to Joy"; "Graphic America—the Shakers"; "Psyche"; "Keepsake"; "Maya"; "Between the angels"; and of course the title poem, "An Animal Of The Sixth Day."

What drew me to Laura Fargas' poems in journals were the delight of their attitude, their tone of celebration, the rich details and sounds, the surprise of exciting closure. Waiting for the manuscript to arrive in this first-book series, I wondered if she could sustain such a tone toward much of this fleeting world. And yes, I discovered, she can. I'm touched that we could be so lucky to publish this wonderful book. Laura Fargas' poems are abundant reward for hours of toil, giving up time I could have spent with friends and family. Her poems astonish and thrill me.

The first poem of hers I found in a journal was "Timshel." So much of what I read a poem for is here: specifics and sounds that delight me;

unexpected but persuasive turns toward ever more delightful details; and a closure that lets me walk away with more than I imagined or hoped to find—all of it new, in my own language, but linked more richly than I ever thought mere words could capture. With each reading, I feel the cheer and excitement I found in her way of expressing hopes and joys we all long for.

Look at how she brings joy even by shaping the book's beginning and end: the book begins in "Timshel" as one long rush, without stanzas, and closes with the pure satisfaction of a poem of seven seven-line stanzas, a crescendo, a symphony's finale.

"Let be be finale of seem," Wallace Stevens wrote, and Richard Wilbur wrote "Love calls us to the things of this world." To an animal of the sixth day, the things of this world, like Stevens' ice cream, are absolute good, and craving them all is "part of the gift"—"the cigarette, the beer, the cold swim in the lake" ("Timshel"). "How much I love it all," she insists, knowing "no one has yet triangulated You."

The poems of Laura Fargas embrace this lovely and various world, like the affirmations of James Wright, who also loved this world, this "rifted paradise." I think of the marvelous insight of James Dickey's comment in *Sorties* about Roethke: "When you read him, you realize with a great surge of astonishment and joy that, truly, you are not yet dead."

She embraces it all, or certainly a generously inclusive sampling, in poems Zen and Christian, Greek and Talmudic. She's aware of risk; it is no easy grace she gives us. Laura once said, "Roethke says 'I trust all joy' in his notebooks—a dangerous and serious stance."

Craft earns her stance; craft makes these poems feel true—the stanzas and line breaks, the repetition of images, rhythms, and sounds. I love flying, a matter of life or death; but a well-wrought poem yields insights and joy I find nowhere else. The poems of Laura Fargas go a long way toward answering the old questions: *What does poetry do? What is it for?* Her poems express for me much of the splendor we all need, a sense of wonder and recognition and hope.

I love the way she loves this world, this "rifted paradise." In "Peris," her poem about those beautiful, fairylike beings in Persian mythology, she recalls an epiphany in school, "how the grape dipped in liquid nitrogen / shattered," and how the shocked students, "griefstricken," realized "what that meant for every physical thing, / including ourselves." I think of the ending of Hopkins' "Spring and Fall: for a Young Child" ("It is the blight man was born for, / it is Margaret you mourn for").

Whatever we are, we are, and these poems accept and embrace and celebrate. In spite of, or because of it all, her poem concludes: "Yet even breaking, the body / is what I want, its teeth, its crooked shadows" ("Peris").

The book opens with a voice reading us our rights—but not as if under arrest, but as we are, animals of the sixth day, here on this amazing earth. Her poems offer a new start from now, this moment, wherever we are. *An Animal of the Sixth Day*—that striking title—has another companion sub-title, a poem near the book's end: "in which she loves everything." *Ah?* I probably asked. *Proof?* For I expect every poem to show me, to earn its extravagant claims. And she does, ending, "If a watermelon seed takes root in the sink, / she drinks bathroom water for weeks." I put my hand over my mouth and nod, grinning gladly to myself, believing every word.

From mathematics to physics, from Leonardo to Van Gogh, from Kyoto to the Shakers—even when she tries "not to think"—always there is "Beauty Beauty Beauty" ("Natural Selection"). Bold and disarmingly charming, she won't let go of splendor "like a small / gray hound tagging at its heels. Love is forever / in dog years" ("Doggy Doggerel"). In this deliciously risky and witty poem, she speaks maybe for us all, and for all of these tough and lovely poems: "If this be rank sentimentality / (and it is), make the most of it." In a poem for Howard Nemerov that begins "The easy sentimentalism I'm ready with. . .," she says, "Weather without grandeur, chum, but we'll take it / exactly as is, as always" ("Howard").

Laura Fargas knows the world is not an unrifted paradise, and the closing simile of "Timshel" is not Prometheus unbound or Sisyphus freed, but merely mortal: "I may shiver amid the stripes of rain / like a wet marmot in a zoo." The poem's tone is not bitterness, though, or loathing, but outrageous acceptance and celebration, a wild gratitude for this fleeting world where we have certain rights to enjoy, to take time to breathe, to do the simple work we do without hurry or remorse: "You may eat the fruit in wonderment." Sometimes, "My job is to watch leaves fall" ("Out Of Time"). At other times, "But thank you anyway, I may pray. I may spend / all of tomorrow trying to rehang a leaf" ("Timshel"). So much freedom is breathless; in that poem, feel the pause after "Please":

> remembering also how much I want. Please,
> I may say, this giddy greed is part of the gift.

Feel the pause, the enchanting emphasis of "Listen":

> Listen
> how copiously the world is raining these permissions,
> and how wisely the grass is drinking them down.
> Listen to the roof dripping as roofs should,

IX

and to the lantern cover faithfully
keeping the finch nest dry, though its
eggs have hatched and flown.

("Timshel")

Most poems in this book have seven lines, and I assume she worked intentionally with that length as a form. When I saw her love of seven lines, I asked myself, What better way to express, through simple form, the privilege and hope for this animal of the sixth day—seven, that ancient cardinal number, meaning variously perfection or good luck.

As I wrote that paragraph, I heard through our open windows high in an oak tree the high-pitched *chip, chip* of cardinals my wife and I watched earlier that morning building their nest. More amazing happy accidents like this happen than we can jot down—but there are never enough gifts like these poems, these lovely, thrilling things Laura Fargas has made. Whether she found them easily or worried each poem through hundreds of drafts, when I read them, the lines seem as natural as birdsong, and that is what I admire about craft. They charm me with intense and joyful experience, and each time I read, they open the vivid and sensuous world.

Craft, I claimed, is what lifts these poems out of mere expressions of a happy heart into made things even I can be glad for. Twice, she adapts her seven-line form in longer poems that gather power, "Slow-Match" and "Of-A-Shadow Dream Man," like other long poems she sustains ("Timshel," for instance; "Transmission"; "Graphic America—the Shakers"; and the title poem).

In this collection—even with some words I had to look up and gladly tried to retain (*timshel, peris*)—Laura Fargas celebrates creation in the natural language I love—those tasty, common words she accepts and makes uncommon in context, always of this earth but almost holy: *passion, sassafras, hosannas.* I'm amazed at how she makes sounds redouble and explode in such simple and right ways of saying, lines that seem not made at all, but natural and easy to read. Read aloud, for example, these sounds in the opening poem:

cheery *yes*es that rattle on the sidewalk at our feet
like beads popped off a string. I may do
what I have done. I may smash the hollow rock
without breaking stride and splinter the glitter inside
all over a midnight street. . . .
. . . . . . . . . . . . . . .
I may mention to God now and then how much I love it all.

("Timshel")

Frost claimed that a poem "begins in delight and ends in wisdom," and the poems of Laura Fargas arrive at more than I thought I would find, leaving me excited and satisfied, nothing more to be said. Consider the earned and startling closures of "Timshel"; "Irises" "Barely Husbanding Their Own Bodies"; "Out of Time"; "October-struck"; "Ode to Joy"; "Transmission"; "Graphic America—the Shakers"; "Perfection Had Ten Names While In Its Body"; "An Animal Of The Sixth Day"; and the ending of "Of-A-Shadow Dream Man," the finale to all this music, as beautiful a closure as I could hope for.

The title "Timshel" in the opening poem was sub-titled *"Thou Mayest"* when published in *The Georgia Review*. It reminds me of the crucial discussion of God's message to Cain in Steinbeck's version of Genesis 4 in *East of Eden*, which eventually provides the hope of redemption for tormented Cal, played by James Dean in the first movie version.

Steinbeck's old men struggle with versions of the text of Genesis. One version commands Cain the brother killer, *"do thou rule over* him [sin]"—a burden that doesn't satisfy them ("What a great burden of guilt men have!" Lee cries out); another version promises *"thou shalt,"* which strips Cain of free will. The old men conclude with fascination that the Hebrew word *"timshel"* is better translated *"thou mayest"*—which is the key, gives us a choice, the free will that lets us be called truly human. "Think of the glory of the choice!" Lee insists, saying, "I have a new love for that glittering instrument, the human soul. . . . It is always attacked and never destroyed—because 'Thou mayest'" (*East of Eden,* chapters 22 and 24).

Even if we are not gods but merely what Pindar in the last poem says we are ("though what he says / we are is drift, wist and want"), Laura Fargas loves it all, as her opening poem proposes and the last poem holds to, even

> particles, smaller

than the smallest nouns?
Not even quarks, charmed or colorful,
but the bits of dust that glitter,
falling very slowly in the light.

> ("Of-A-Shadow Dream Man")

## Gerard Manley Hopkins found hope in spite of loss:

And though the last lights off the black West went
    Oh, morning, at the brown brink eastward, springs—
Because the Holy Ghost over the bent
    World broods with warm breast and with ah! bright wings.

> ("God's Grandeur")

In the poems of Laura Fargas' world, I find mystery and magic, also, in the everyday—marvelous because they are so natural, so purely there:

Starlings flash by my office window
every day during the blue hour,
headed west in groups that move
inside themselves, obeying no rule
I can see. . . . . . .
. . . . . . . . . .
Things move.  Very small things
move and move, at breathless speeds,
swarming past our eyes invisibly.

("Of-A-Shadow Dream Man")

Her poems discover for me all over again that perhaps, perhaps the fondest gift of being "an animal of the sixth day" and having "certain rights" is the gift of seeing how delicious it all is—the natural, mystical world, so glorious in paradox and fleetingly available, now, within reach.

There, across the coast road,
where the pelicans fish by crashing.  They just stop
flying and fall.

("Irises")

The book's structure is like an arc.  Whatever books she may live to write, this one feels done.  She begins her collection with freedom and the joy of music, of strumming "a zither."  In the end ("Of-A-Shadow Dream Man"), thinking of starlings flashing by her office window, she leaves us with this simple, breathtaking image of freedom, of doing simply, and with all the heart, whatever is given:

How purely themselves things are,
like starlings dodging on the wind,
headed from food to sleep, rising
and falling without the thought
this is what wings are for.

Walter McDonald
Series Editor

# Contents

# II

III

# An Animal of the Sixth Day

I

# Timshel

You have certain rights.  You may
strum a zither.  You may return to the key
that plinks a little flat over and over,
and call the piano tuner back.
You may eat the fruit in wonderment at its cleanly
interior, and rub the juice deeply into the skin
of your hands.  From the sassafras,
you may have one of each of the three shapes of leaf,
and in different colors, too.  Listen
how copiously the world is raining these permissions,
and how wisely the grass is drinking them down.
Listen to the roof dripping as roofs should,
and to the lantern cover faithfully
keeping the finch nest dry, though its eggs
have hatched and flown.  You may be Winston Churchill
pottering in oil paint and brooding over navies.
You may be the stocky monk with poor eyesight
taking a month to rubricate the letter 'S.'
These are the opposites of commandments,
cheery *yes*es that rattle on the sidewalk at our feet
like beads popped off a string.  I may do
what I have done.   I may smash the hollow rock
without breaking stride and splinter the glitter inside
all over a midnight street.  I may have

the cigarette, the beer, the cold swim in the lake.
I may mention to God now and then how much I love it all,
remembering also how much I want.  Please,
I may say, this giddy greed is part of the gift.
I may say the universe is big and full of both fullness and
starry voids, and no one has yet triangulated You.
But thank you anyway, I may pray.  I may spend
all of tomorrow trying to rehang a leaf.
I may shiver amid the stripes of rain
like a wet marmot in a zoo.

# Canopy

Somehow the wind is touching them one by one,
the high trees, spreading their leaves
and swaying their long stems gently and singly.
They are flowers after all.  They are
that shy and malleable.  There is no one to pick them,
and even if their high shivering could be a kind of asking-for,
there can be no taking to accept their grace.

# Peris

Spirits of the air, subsisting on perfumes.
Griefstricken, we dream of being dream-things,
undiseased, vacant, philosophical.  Remember from school
how the grape dipped in liquid nitrogen
shattered?  And what that meant for every physical thing,
including ourselves?  Yet even breaking, the body
is what I want, its teeth, its crooked shadows.

*for Pat Gilfillan*

8

# Grass The Fine Body Hairs Of Earth

My shorthand for it is *passion is holy*.
We can live inside the lilies-of-the-field text.
Watching gulls startle off the ground
as if hundreds of lashing wings are our native air.
Breathe in wings, exhale speckled orange wildflowers.
Eyes, elbows, tears : suns, mountains, rivers.
Lovemaking rings with hosannas.

*for William Matthews*

# Barely Husbanding Their Own Bodies

Will tomorrow be the harsh afternoon
when the saint remembers his mother's bread
and cries in his cave?  Will a seraph
crouch invisibly at that man's stone hearth
watching, wondering what blood is?
Will a sign come to requite the unleavened years?
A bird to sing, a few strangers in blue robes?

# Slow-Match

The black hair and the pale-beer gold mixed on their pillows,
it crossed my mind, it did.  She came next, and she
caught the golden ring the previous ex
threw out a taxicab's window into the filth—
'it's not the dirt, it's the *filth*'—
of the world that didn't have his heart in it.
I remember that heart, and his knees, caught in the light

of our last naked morning together,
and the red sag of his balls behind his skinny calves
as he drew those knees up.
So that blondeheaded woman couldn't keep him, or he her,
or either of them themselves, who knows—
so much self-knowledge and not enough self, it comes
glibly to my tongue.  Let me never utter

a cheesy gag about that man except in love,
never unless there is a slow smoky tune and a slow
smoky wine in the room along with it,
and that glass raised to his health.
And to his difficult heart, his difficult knees,
the looping tangle of his erudition—
slow-match, they called it, the first foot or two of fuse,

slow-match so they could step away, so they could judge
the burning and the angle of the cannon-pot
and rush back in to stamp out an erroneous flame
if need be, and need sometimes was—
because once the flame reached the quick-match braid
the explosion had as good as happened, the mortar
as good as landed, the fort as good as blown—

and to say 'as good as' can mean 'as bad as,'
like wood that's not only green but sitting out in rain.
But some people live only by the light of such fires,
and so we take it, we burn wet resiny pine and punk board,
and each time the heart, that slow red ember,
rekindles, we give it a log.

# Irises

Imagine him imagining the painting.
So many small strokes, to be generous as flowers themselves.
As if even though less is more, more can also be more,
kinder.  It helps these irises escape
back into the wild lavishness of flower root, grass seed,
that life still happening.  There, across the coast road,
where the pelicans fish by crashing.  They just stop
flying and fall.

# Medieval skies. Rectilinear stars

Medieval skies.  Rectilinear stars on royal blue.
Sometimes *angeli musicantes* with krumhorn,
psalter, lute.  Their hair belled out, weightless like
Judy Reznik's as she grins at us from orbit,
twirling in zero-G some tiny instrument for splitting
spectra from the million minute rays delicately
gold-leafed tangent to each star.

# If there is a

If there is a God, he has a lot to answer for.
Crocuses, purple cups that bloom through snow.
Cerulean, cornflower, azure, turquoise, ultramarine.
Mist off round haybales along the Sand Road
just after 5 a.m., when the foxes go to ground.
Not only the obvious evils, but also these other things
we should not mistake for easy.

# Living In Is

Hardly a waft remains of the skunk's stink
an hour or two after dawn,
though at 3 a.m., the sharp little quarrel
enveloped the house.
Now the grass, the sandy soil, the fir's bark
have only a small stale smell
one must be looking for.
If all anger sluiced away like that.
If change tried itself out, and yielded
without leaving damage.
If the bent tree, unbent, releafed the same year
and the child could sustain a kindness
for her parents. If *if* did not also mean *then*.
If wanting rose without shame and subsided
without wistfulness. Would the proverb
then say, *Vengeance is a dish without spice?*
We say of skunks they have malign little eyes.
They trundle their elegant fur
through the shrubs and do not wish to be seen
or touched. They have no if,
living in is. Sniffing the chemical trace,
I imagine the animal

safely asleep now somewhere nearby.

If it dreams.  If it relives

its outraged squeak.  If it lives.  If it dies.

If the season, the fir tree, the grass.  If I.

If God.  If the starry night spins past without shame.

# Harpist

*2600 BC, from Teke near Knossos*

My version is at night.
That you barely know your instrument,
that you look away,
look up at an angle that closes your throat.
You are not singing,
you are not letting the olive wood and sheepgut
see your sadness.  You look at stars,
the harsh brilliancy that mantles Crete at nightfall,
unclenching only at the pale red touch of dawn.
You will be three hundred generations in the ground before
the great singer makes dawn's tinged fingers famous.
Like me your silent beginning.
Like me searching for a note, five notes.
There is no asking the stars, cold eminences.
There is not yet the intimacy of looking down
to the frame and strings of the harp.
Black and white, your face and the night sky,
severe and absolute, both of them.
The music, where is it?  The harp curves on your hands
like a girl who is willing.
Her poetry is waiting to be written, stirring like lemon scent
when the sun heats the fruit.
It's dark, I know that sky.  It's painful

not to look at the harp in your hands.

That angle of your jaw, the whiteness of the neck

bent back, a cut throat exposure.

The stars don't bother to pinch one life away from this earth.

They aren't even waiting.  It is the harp,

your hand on its frame, your hand at the strings, that waits,

hungering for the huge, the next.

# Valhalla

The dead remember the smell of bread,
what it was like when the orange orchards
west of town bloomed into the breeze.
They remember conversation, they try to talk.
Gambling, sex, riddles.  Grasping at
the sound of one cricket under the steps.
They don't know why exactly.

# At Poplar Pond

There are angels right there between those trees.
Don't be frightened, I'm not seeing things.
The spaces we call empty are full of—
not tree, not sky, but us. We station our angels
aloft to mark our place in the holy ordinariness.
So these simples—chalky water, poplar,
moth-flown light—are that blind, sacred flesh.

# "The Battle For Peace Has Begun"

*ad for Star Trek VI*

Accretion, not force.  Not the waterfall,
but way upriver the trickled source.
People who mill grain, compile herbals,
have time to grind van Leeuwenhoek's lens.
Who'll find the red dye in onion skins.
I spent all day doing nothing, outdoors.
Don't call that my war.

# Word Up

Some days apologizing to each several leaf.
The cannibal nature of my looking.
Shuffling phenomena into shapeliness
before—no before—imposing *before.*
*Lovers* leaves me, sliding a last kiss
along my tongue. Say *awe.* Say
*grandeur, flamingo, caress*—twice, thrice.

# Out Of Time

My job is to watch leaves fall.
To watch the falling leaves and to read
the autobiography of a beautiful girl who became
rich and sad.  And thinking of her
without disdain, to see how the squirrel
replaces the earth once he has stored food.
The moon arced up and shrank
in last night's warm, foggy sky, and I saw her
twinned in a silted lake four hours or so
before dawn.  I watched a few degrees of her arc
and came under the trees to listen
to the rest of the night, leaf by leaf.  The beautiful girl
was still waiting in 1964 where I'd left her
and another sad thing happened soon.
The moon's blue settled into darkness
and the other blue rose at the top of the trees
and an owl cried out and the lichens and the leaves
became visible.  Leaves are not
numberless, just as almost nothing is truly random.
But I am not the angel who enumerates
all rising, all falling, all the births and death
no one sees.  To me, the leaves seem
like prime numbers, wholly golden and indivisible
in their infinite series.  I cannot say

which one leaf will come down next.
I cannot tell you how the beautiful girl's story
came out, since she is still alive.
Whatever this is, is not what it is to be
a tree or the recording angel, but this moveless,
unpowerful condition is something good.
Even magnificent. I can say that. I can say
there is no end to the soft falling.

# October-struck

And then in the falling comes a rising,
as of the bass coming up for autumn's last insects
struggling amid the mosaic of leaves on the lake's surface.
We express it as the season of lacking, but what is this
        nakedness—
the unharvested corn frost-shriveled but still a little golden
under the diffuse light of a foggy sky,
the pin oak's newly stark web of barbs, the woodbine's vines
shriven of their scarlet and left askew in the air
like the tangle of threads on the wall's side
of the castle tapestry—what is it but greater intimacy,
the world slackening its grip on the veils, letting them slump
to the floor in a heap of sodden colors, and saying,
this is me, this is my skeletal muscle,
my latticework of bones, my barren winter skin, this is it
and if you love me, know that this is what you love.

II

# Ode to Joy

*after Gustav Klimt's 'Beethoven frieze'*

Lovers the grit on which Paradise pearls,
"this kiss for the whole world."
Passion burns inside redemption, on the same plane
with the choir of heavenly angels, who praise
God with linked hands and closed eyes.
Rapture rises from that kiss in a golden steam
mere suns and moons swim through.

# Transmission

*in the Zen tradition, the name for*
*a master's formal recognition that*
*the student is qualified to teach*

—a hurried knock—
patient teaching—the unseen slither
of a virus in its elegant spirals—from here to there.
Me to you.  This gift.  Never mind, don't take it.
At the monastery, it's not the moss or the walls
or the mats or the thin tea that care
whether the bee springs up inside you
dancing the dance on wings that says
*there is honey-stuff over there, come, come, come,*
*you are one of me and if I tell you*
*oriented by where the sun sits above that flower,*
*you will understand and come.*
It's not the moss that cares, and the masters themselves
care so obscurely that the hurt of it is great.
It's one of the teachings, the mystery of love at the roots.
Everything resolves into an example:  the speckled leaf,
this morning chill and your breath like a frost cloud,
and oh, that thin tea.  You hold it,
wanting deeply.  The leaf crisps, the cloud disperses,
the tea gets cold.  They don't turn back.
Memory seems like a hurt.  (Do you understand

it's your freckles I'm writing about,

the soft lapping of hair at the nape of your neck,

your personal music of wordless sounds?)

Memory is a hurt all day long, some days.

And the mind says, how can I get to the honey,

how get the bee to kiss the flower?  The mind knows it can't.

They are all there, the bee, the flower, the sun,

the moment that shakes body and soul to a great Ah!

The mind knows the word 'transmission,'

memory clings to the story of the master who says,

*What is the Buddha?—dry shit on a stick—*

There is no moving that implacable bee, the insect

science says can't fly but does.

It will rise or it won't, but you

must be ready every moment for that dance

to jump up inside you.  You must always be good enough

to be all the other bees, the ones summoned,

the ones that understand the directions in terms of the sun

even on wholly cloudy days, that rise

to go to flowers and drink, whose nature

is to go to flowers and drink and dance and tell others.

# Wave & Particle

Herons hunt at the marsh edge,
lacking the mind to desire abstractions.
What I take boating in the bright fog
is my need to be seen by them, to feel
the ice of the moon melting on my palms.
Round as a kiss, sharp as a bullet,
light soaks the slow event.

# Natural Selection

Ten feet under off Corfu, I opened
my eyes into uttermost blue.
Beauty Beauty Beauty, I tried not to think.
Awakened by lightning, mouth agape
not to drink but to breathe, a fish, a fetus,
I drifted inert toward the crawl ashore,
doomed to evolve in the dirt.

# Pythagoras Hated $\sqrt{2}$

It was no integer, no sure sign
mind could lift the difficult fog
veiling the true truth about the real reality.
A dodecahedron, now *that* he could plausibly
link to the Quintessence.  Radical two
loomed like his grave, real and irrational
as hunters' hands painting a cave.

# "Winter, Leper of the World"

*after Roualt*

I can't really tell if winter
is a dark massive angel burdened
with wings, or a man hefting a big sack,
the kind in folktales where the woodcutter
hauls the wolf.  But how heavy we are,
how hard it is to carry us across the peak
of the still time—that I see.

# "Graphic America— the Shakers"

*London Graphic, May 14, 1870*

No rug, no curtains at the windows,
no ornaments in their daughters' hair.
It would be against God's pleasure
if the grainy wood yielded a splinter.
They move in two circles, males and females,
hands cupped before them to catch

whatever grace may be shed to this room.
Their feet slide, their bonnets catch and lose shadows.
So little is visible—plain dress, plain window,
broadly planked floor—yes, the Invisible
might sink down gratefully to this room,
the way the skeins of swans following

their high route to the south will descend
to a large enough pond for a day or two.
What a sweet sound is theirs—
the smack of their landing in the marsh,
not to sing their fabled requiem but to preen
and squabble in their ordinary fashion.

The Shakers, after whispering
blessings in each others' ears—the women

kiss each other, but not the men—resume their rows,
again raise their pale palms and commence,
while circling around three brethren and three sisters
who stand singing hymns and psalms,

"a curious hopping dance." Oh what joy,
to lift the body off the heavy, grasping earth
sheerly for the sake of pleasing God.
How sure not of salvation but of blessedness
those six voices would have sounded.
What angel was not watching in this century

when their final meeting came to pass
and disbanded with some last few leaps?
And the swans, dipping their bills
in the marshwater, coming up dripping with algae,
what does the south offer them,
what whisper in the muscles of their wings says to rise?

## Perfection Had Ten Names
## While In Its Body

Awake with his death sentence in a lightless garden.

Married to the necessity of that murder.

The perfect diamond has no burden, only its mute

witness to the powers of earth.

A different force held that young man.

So moved he opened his body to the nail.

# The First Elegy

Reading five translations at once
reminds me of a problem I love
and will never solve: trisecting an angle
with compass and ruler.  You can see the answer,
but not prove it.  Rilke waits
at the vanishing point where angles and angels
greet the accurate heart.

# The Going Poem

Tomorrow I'll light a candle for your journey,
its safety in the ordinary way.
Today, you saw.  The leaves so thick there is
no road to touch.  The sky dull gray,
nothing to romanticize there.  On the desk,
a waterlogged and dried copy of Leonardo's notebooks,
the index open to 'the olfactory
mechanism of a lion.'  Insatiable, he opened
a lion, and he looked into its blackness
carefully.  We can see in the face
of the old man's self portraits some of what
looked back.  He gives us something crucial,
yet to have it, it seems we must also find it ourselves
in our separate lives.  And what is that *it,*
the irreducible that hides in pronouns and particles,
that strong *something?*  The rightness in the body
of bowing to a woman's grave, speaking of gratitude.
The old rice-planters at the crossroads near Kyoto,
clapping to waken a god to receive his honors.
What the lioness smells, amber in tall amber grass,
empty-bellied.  What these are examples of I can't define,
though I can tell I don't want to leave it, and want

it not to leave me.  Cold sky, cold cabin slowly warming.
The day's food in a bag in the car.  The green flame
of lichen on the pine minute by minute
less visible in the blue.

*for Jane Hirshfield*

# For Her

Here I am in Paradise, wishing I were in love instead.
Animals scamper past with almost no fear,
splashing from high branch to high branch on the trees.
But me, I read the sour poem Abelard
supposedly wrote his Eloise, encountering rumors
of her whoredom wherever he took his mutilated body
to try to teach. He knew, perhaps,
not to reproach, but to mourn. *Must you, when we*
*were such lovers? Must you use the cup*
*into which we dripped the dew from rose petals and drank*
*that rare intoxication, must you*
*let that cup now hold a cider sold for pennies a dip?*
Oh Eloise, perhaps we should have died,
you and I, right then when we were loved, however young.
Abelard cannot understand, though he is stuck
in the resin of your century and I am afloat
eight hundred years later in the rising flush
of my blood along the skin of my shoulders, neck, all down
the spine, all down the hips.
What do men imagine? Everything, everything.
And so do we, and going to live in a garden,
as for example the well-tended convent where Abelard
preferred to imagine you, is not enough.
Better to live by your truth, to let the rumors

be passed, to live by the savor of subtle flowers

even if their pungency and rose-red fire

is not the same thing as love,

as we cannot help but relearn each day.

# A Night When Only Angels Interest Me

Dipping into our times, as we slip a naked foot
into water.  Awkward in the strange clothing of flesh,
sent to wrestle and falsely lose, to slap
Tobias' eyes with a fish.  To tell the Marys,
"he is gone, he is not here."
How do they see our hunting loneliness?
I wonder at their first instant of existence,
in which each one knows whether it will cleave.
Wonder if the falling believe themselves tragic.
If in angelic intelligence quivers anything
a human heart might know for grief.

# Properly concentrated, the moon

Properly concentrated, the moon kindles.
Can catch a little heap of dessicated needles,
fire the snaps out of hardening sap.
The night of my birthday,
earth seemed like water, all water.  I put
his letter in his envelope, sealed, stamped.
Lit it with moonbeams.  First scorch, then flare.

# Stitch in Time

The tick and tock die off
innumerable ways, and what's the chirp
of a hearth cricket to an archeologist?
Still I love all the sound
advice we get, like Tolstoi's "make it
strange," or the dying Keynes' "I
should have drunk more champagne."

# I like it when

I like it when the sky says *where have you been?*
*Housed in a fist*, I explain, *stuck inside*
*somebody's movie.* *Have I missed too many clouds*
*to ever catch up?* And the sky says *eons ago.*
Not really. The sky says *no.* No, that's me again.
Both those answers could be true, but the sky
is pink and gray and blue and red and wind.

# A Little Champagne Music

Should there be a poetry of men?  "Why do you suppose
everyone's writing about God these days?"
Taffy-colored hair and damselflies, amaryllis
vulgar as a flatted horn, clavicles and happenstance.
We should be coupling and uncoupling like the Atchison,
Topeka, and the Santa Fe.  Our daily bread
and foxtrot.  And a-one and a-two . . .

*for Gerald Stern*

# Doggy Doggerel

When my dog Sallie said *woof*
she meant it, and she was always right.
Woof is us, while warp's the rough inner weave
holding splendor together like a small
gray hound tagging at its heels.  Love is forever
in dog years.  If this be rank sentimentality
(and it is), make the most of it.

# The Gift

This is the color this shingle is, seven years
after being set in a northern climate
on a southfacing roof, midmorning of a cloudy day
after heavy rain at night.  And this
is the color of this long pine needle
in the first half-minute after it falls
on the knee of a brown-haired woman.
At Ryoanji, at the north edge of the garden,
there is a wall of a hundred colors
no one names.
The white pebbles that are the sea or the sky
or your soul as it ought to be,
these the monks presume to rake in the dawn hours
into lines as straight as some of the world's lies
and into waves eddying around the stones,
including, you are allowed to know,
around the invisible one.
The wall is just the wall, the untouched rim of the absolute.
The colors come from inside,
flowering from centuries of centuries and no touch.
Somewhere in the clay and the making,
there was oil; the rest is rain
and the long unraveling we call chance.
Blue-gray-green,

I could tell you, or I could pry loose the slate
and the time of day and this slant of half-light
and carry them to you.
Would you accept them from my hand?

III

# An Animal Of The Sixth Day

It was not that Cain yielded.
Midrash says that after Abel panicked and ran,
Cain chased him
from hill to mountaintop, from mountaintop to valley,
from one world to the other,
and when they struggled,
it was Abel who gained a death-hold,
and Abel who was deaf like God to cries for mercy,
except that Cain finally said
'when you return alone, you will strike them into mourning.'
And for Adam's sake, and Eve's, Abel let go.
And Cain, like an animal of the fifth day
that cannot suffer pity, struck with a heavy rock.
God marked his face,
and Eve brought forth another son
so that murder would not be our only parent.
Midrash also teaches that we are not
to contemplate the mystery of creation, not to reach
our hearts into the mute soul
of the unpeopled world and follow the fire into Adam's bones,
unless we are ourselves alone as Adam.
Now while I green my soul in solitude
with the songs of crickets and frogs,
I am not even to wonder at the infinitesimal splash
of father into mother that shot me here like an arrow

until I am that thing, alone as Adam.
It is a paradox, it cannot be. Adam by nature
lacked the thing his second son died for,
a certain pity for his parents. Adam sizzled
into full attention, alive on the clay he was made of,
with the beasts leaning forward to sniff at
the scorched air and watch the new one
with their paradisal eyes. Piety, joy,
the easy pleasure of standing up that first time,
whatever Adam's kind of aloneness was,
it is not mine. All one. All one.
Adam was born at the cusp of manyness,
born at the beginning of the long fall
down to trillions and quadrillionths we measure so well.
Eve was the end of the all-one. Eve was
the beginning of me, particulate
amid the dazzle of changing leaves,
dense with pity for all of us, the mother in the south,
the father in the north, leaves of the striped maple
and sugar maple, needles of the Douglas fir, myself, myself—
no. I want to be this, bespattered with the falling,
charged with the glory and retained grace
of a destructible world. I want to be
an animal of the sixth day.

# Translated Either As 'Experience' Or 'Suffering'

In the *Agamemnon*, wisdom comes dripping
like saline on a cancer ward.
Approaching what is merciless in us with mercy,
following pain back like a red thread toward its source.
Some say it's a matter of noticing we're already inside.
*Pathei mathos.* Something teaches us. The moth at the lamp,
the lesson braided in the wick.

# Howard

The easy sentimentalism I'm ready with is,
*You taught me silla, a little blue lily.*
Souls are a sort of climate, flowers a luck
above our coaxing.  Today's sky seems shallow,
metallic, its clouds dirty and vague.
Weather without grandeur, chum, but we'll take it
exactly as is, as always.

*in mem. Howard Nemerov, 5 vii 1991*

# Psyche

Whatever it is, it goes out of reach.
Might as well turn into butterflies,
as she did.  Veneration of the empty house
is a lonesome mania—flowers for Valentino
year after year, full-blown roses
shriveling above a body the giver never touched.

# Speaking

Not with the tongues of men and of angels,
not me.  Can't even always be with love,
easy as love is late at night, remembering the dead.
I'd like to write a book that angels love to read
because it's what human beings have to say.
Washing all the windows on the first day in a new house,
cooking spaghetti in the only clean pot.

*for Li-Young Lee*

# Reflecting What Light We Can't Absorb

Sing, choirs. We waken into this fire
simple as crickets, our own light
blurred in the sparkle of particulars.
Leaf, leaf, leaf, leaf, leaf.
Somewhere in the transparency between
sun behind it and the greenness in my mind,
the lessons of grass ignite.

# Keepsake

I forgot to notice the fate of my favorite apple leaf,
the one that arched with a spreading stain
growing gradually seasonal as the disease enlarged.
It kept not falling from one noon to the next,
though all the healthy leaves around it yellowed and dropped.
It's raining here.  The mockingbird this morning
started out with a bluejay cry, a northern harshness
that still sounds just right in my ears.
Ochres and siennas, the fires of southern fall
burning all around.  The trees bronzing,
with that word's false sense of stillness and keeping.
What keeps?  Milk, only briefly, eggs, bread,
all the simples.  Keep well.  Memory's
like wine; it might keep, it might turn.  Sometimes
what we keep is the mockingbird version of a jay,
but I say that's lovable too, and the disease
that made the apple leaf orange as any maple's,
admirable.  The apple leaf is no less real
than any of our city oaks; it's we who say
all the female ginkgos in Brooklyn are lonely.
The trees are in the business of leaves.
There is no unreal leaf anywhere in the world.
There is nowhere where everything I said to you
isn't the straight truth.

# in which she loves everything

Her own dun skin and the shell that scratched it white,
dusky seaside sparrows, now extinct; olivine basalt—
everything that ever was, for its was-ness.
Tableaux vivants, those aristos in their powder
pretending to be a painting.  Grown-out potato eyes.
If a watermelon seed takes root in the sink,
she drinks bathroom water for weeks.

# Maya

So much comes into the world veiled.
A dawn lake,
a white mushroom that carries its earth up in a cup.
Veiled children will be the ones to flip the arcane cards
spelling out mysteries for the rest of us
to believe or blink away,
whose fine-boned hands will sense when a stick
is eager to go through the caul of land to the water below.
We dance with veils,
we choose them as a metaphor of our blindness
to the single radiance that all things are.
Each blade of grass.  Each star-nosed mole,
each morel and coral and russala.
The morning lake shifts under its veil
like a shy blue thought of luck.  Inside,
the fish are cold and still, have not warmed yet
to today's hunger.  The yellow leaves
drifting down to star its surface
are emblems of nothing, just leaves.  Each leaf.
I am just one woman shivering in wet air
trying to love every variety of light
without yielding to some other blindness.
So cold.  The rock damp, the log damp,
the world born fresh, wet, veiled in light.
Each fish, each fly, each of the nineteen

strands of gossamer the spider has made
to enlace her wet web.  Each fish.
Each spider.  Each woman.  Each veil
that sighs gently to the floor as the girl,
her eyes aglitter, whirls through barefoot spirals
of revealing and revealing more and keeping
her heart for herself.

*for Dianne Wickes*

# Palos Verdes High School

Staring out to sea.  Not usefully,
not to say 'cumulus' or 'brine' or 'typhoon,'
just staring and having the wind
come up the cliff or over the sand
and blow grit in my eyes.
Wiping the grit out and looking some more.
Not looking for anything but glad to see.

# Between the angels

Between the angels who peel our hearts
and the ones gnawing steadily inward
comes the stolid oath that holds us fast
to the world of apple and fire.
And the heart wants something to be kind to,
even if only a fish to sprinkle
crumbs on the water for once or twice a day.

# Kuan Yin

Of the many buddhas I love best the girl
who will not leave the cycle of pain before anyone else.
It is not the captain declining to be saved
on the sinking ship, who may just want to ride his shame
out of sight.  She is at the brink of never being hurt again
but pauses to say, *All of us. Every blade of grass.*
She chooses to live in the tumble of souls through time.
Perhaps she sees spring in every country,
talks quietly with farm women while helping to lay seed.
Our hearts are a storm she trembles at.  I picture her
leaning on a tree or humming or joining a volleyball game
on Santa Monica beach.  Her skin shines with sweat.
The others may not know how to notice what she does to
     them.
She is not a fish or a bee; it is not pity or thirst;
she could go, but here she is.

*for Stuart Joseph*

# Absolute Location

That love is a well you could fall down forever.
Ultimately finding stars, and fire-winged angels.
Once I read Euclid in his own language,
drew with my young fingers his austere lines.
Simplicity, but not to fall out of the body,
must be the form of survival and joy.
Measures, as we say of both music and precaution.

*for Linda Gregg*

# Among Our Great Ceremonies

A serious love touches the universe,
the two and one of it contributing to the sum of what's real.
Not that planets or even hydrogen atoms
begin falling toward you, yet something intensifies
where you are.  The different light
shed by double stars.  No consensus why they form,
nor how they'll dim or dazzle, perishing.

*for Jack Gilbert*

# "The Beauty Of Nature
Is The Silence Of God"

*Claude Lansmann,* Shoah

To whom I say thank you for the strange meal of your flesh.
The scent of whose hair answers the scandal of matter.
Who sees man see the fall of the last dusky seaside sparrow,
hovers in white turkeys and headstalled calves.
Thank you for breeding in captivity.
Thank you the ones who survive the unthinkable
for singing again.

# The Problem Of Good

Behind the problem of evil, the problem of good.
The world in its silver-orange light,
pool reflecting seagulls moving hover-dive-hover,
the whole held in stasis by millions of cherry blooms,
pink after pink after white after pink,
tree after tree, inexplicable, yes inexplicable,
never mind your principles of physics.

# Of-A-Shadow Dream Man

He speaks all in nouns, at the limits
of impatience. "Ben. Chevy. Dad.
Dad. LeBaron. Jesse. Ben. Home."
Then teaches us the word for it,
holophrastic. How dense we are in
incomprehension and comprehension alike.
And what about particles, smaller

than the smallest nouns?
Not even quarks, charmed or colorful,
but the bits of dust that glitter,
falling very slowly in the light.
My favorite line in any poem is made
of these, pure particles, all elision.
*ti d' tis; ti d' ou tis;*

What [half a statement] something,
what [the other half] not something?—
"what is man, a man, any man;
and what is he not?" 2000 years
of answers orbit Pindar's asking,
dizzying as the paths of electrons.
And Pindar's own answer, all nouns,

73

*skias onar anthropos*—
"shadow dream man," mating particles
densely with pure noun, as matter
compresses inside the most massive
stars until light itself is too heavy
to get away, though what he says
we are is drift, wist and want.

*Man is but the dream of a shadow.*
Starlings flash by my office window
every day during the blue hour,
headed west in groups that move
inside themselves, obeying no rule
I can see.  Brownian motion seems
as good an explanation as any

for these clouds of birds that pass
through each other like galaxies.
Things move.  Very small things
move and move, at breathless speeds,
swarming past our eyes invisibly.
How fine our understanding is,
the sieve that gives us all at once

quasars and pinpoints, encompasses
shadow and confusion in the text.
How purely themselves things are,

like starlings dodging on the wind,
headed from food to sleep, rising
and falling without the thought
this is what wings are for.

# Notes

Timshel   This word appears in Genesis iv: 7; it is the last thing God
says to Cain before the murder of Abel. John Steinbeck in *East of
Eden* says this word means, "you may, or you may not," that it is
a word implying the need for a choice in the presence of evil.
However, the Israeli poet and scholar Moshe Dor says that
Steinbeck misreads the word, and that it is a simple future tense
of the verb, timshōl: "you will rule."

Peris   Peris are air spirits of Persian mythology, somewhat like
angels, and are portrayed as beautiful, winged girls in Persian
miniatures.

Irises   Van Gogh's painting, which for a time held the record as the
world's most expensive painting, currently hangs in a
not-very-well-lit corner of the Getty Museum in Malibu,
California.

Ode to Joy   Gustav Klimt's 1902 *Beethoven Frieze* has been
painstakingly restored in recent years; the panels are now in the
Osterreichische Gallerie in Vienna and were published in the late
1980's by Skira/Rizzoli. "Diesen Kuss der ganzen Welt"—*this
kiss for the whole world*—is the culminating panel. The phrase
comes from Beethoven's own text, Schiller's *Ode to Joy*.

Transmission   The master who uttered that great, scandalous
teaching was Un-mun, quoted by Seung Sahn in Stephen
Mitchell's *Dropping Ashes on the Buddha*.

Pythagoras Hated √2   Some license is taken in the 'dodecahedron'
part of the poem. It was actually Pythagoras' disciple Philolaus
who linked the Empedoclean elements with the regular solids:
Earth–cube; air–octahedron; fire–tetrahedron; water–
icosahedron; and aether (the fifth element or 'quintessence')–
dodecahedron. See Plato's *Timaeus*, §§ 53-55.

"Winter, Leper of the World"  This Rouault lithograph seems not to be widely published (or perhaps not at all), so I'm particularly grateful to Alan and Nina Weinstein, who first introduced me to it, for letting me visit it several times at their gallery in Iowa City.

Perfection Had Ten Names While In Its Body  Christ is referred to ten different ways in the New Testament.

For Her  In fact, Eloise did become a cloistered nun, but the poem attributed to Abelard (spuriously?) is based on the idea of an Eloise who is still very much in the world.

A Night When Only Angels Interest Me  One of the convolutions of medieval angelology was a doctrine that angels had an instant of free will at the moment of their creation.  Or variantly, that they had an instant of knowledge in which they learned which course they would choose in Lucifer's rebellion.

The Gift  Ryoanji is a Zen monastery in Kyoto, Japan, which is famous for its garden of fifteen stones, of which one can see only fourteen from any given vantage point.

An Animal Of The Sixth Day  Elie Wiesel tells the stories from the Midrash in *Souls on Fire*.

Reflecting What Light We Can't Absorb  The apparent color of a solid, like grass, is that part of the visible spectrum that it can't absorb, and therefore reflects back outward.

Kuan Yin  This is the Chinese name of the bodhisattva known in Japan as Kwannon, in India as Avalokitesvara.  In his translation of Issa, Lewis Mackenzie rendered her name as "she who pauses with her foot on the threshold of Heaven to listen to the cry of distress from earth;" thus, she embodies a quality variously translated as *compassion* or *pity* or *mercy*.  She is said to have appeared in the form of a cloud during the construction of the Buddhist temple Hsi Lai in the San Gabriel Mountains south of Los Angeles.

Absolute Location  The title is a term from Newtonian physics, referring to the non-relativistic concept of Absolute Space in which a thing, such as a star, actually is where it is perceived to be and may reliably be found there again.

Of-A-Shadow Dream Man  The poem quoted is Pindar's *Eighth Nemean Ode*.

The display type is Dauphin, a font created in tribute to George Trump's typeface Delphin I, designed to mirror the script of illuminated manuscripts.

The body type is **Garamond**; Robert Slimbach designed this elegant version of a classic typeface based on specimens, now in the Plantin-Moretus Museum in Antwerp, that were cut, set, and printed by the sixteenth-century French typographer and royal court printer Claude Garamond himself.

The *italics* are based on the type of Robert Granjon, who in the mid-sixteenth century became the first type designer to create italics specifically to harmonize with roman type rather than stand alone.

The numbers are **Caslon,** designed by Carol Twombly, based on the original letter-forms cut in the 1720s by William Caslon.